Kaɪ

How to Visualize Work and Maximize Efficiency and Output with Kanban, Lean Thinking, Scrum, and Agile

Kanban

PUBLISHED BY: Greg Caldwell
© Copyright 2019 - All rights reserved.

The content contained within this book may not be reproduced, duplicated or transmitted without direct written permission from the author or the publisher.

Under no circumstances will any blame or legal responsibility be held against the publisher, or author, for any damages, reparation, or monetary loss due to the information contained within this book. Either directly or indirectly.

Legal Notice:

This book is copyright protected. This book is only for personal use. You cannot amend, distribute, sell, use, quote or paraphrase any part, or the content within this book, without the consent of the author or publisher.

Disclaimer Notice:

Please note the information contained within this document is for educational and entertainment purposes only. All effort has been executed to present accurate, up to date, and reliable, complete information. No warranties of any kind are declared or implied. Readers acknowledge that the author is not engaging in the rendering of legal, financial, medical or professional advice. The content within this book has been derived from various sources. Please consult a licensed professional before attempting any techniques outlined in this book.

By reading this document, the reader agrees that under no circumstances is the author responsible for any losses, direct or indirect, which are incurred as a result of the use of information contained within this document, including, but not limited to, — errors, omissions, or inaccuracies

Greg Caldwell

Table Of Contents

Introduction 6

What Is Work Visualization?...................... 8

Kanban in Action 10

Chapter 1. Kanban As A Way to Visualize Work and Maximize Efficiency and Output 16

Kanban Cards..17

Kanban Columns.......................................19

WIP (Work In Progress) Limits 22

Chapter 2: Lean Thinking............................24

The Workplace..25

Value 26

Value streams...28

Flow..29

Pull 30

Excellence...31

Chapter 3. Agile And Scrum 33

The Benefits Of Going Agile......................34

The 12 Principles 35

Scrum 42

Chapter 4. Why An Organization Needs Kanban: Overlooked Issues That May Cause Massive Problems 48

Poor management..49

Problems with employees 52

Iceberg of Ignorance...54

Poor Customer Service 56

Chapter 5. Taking Control: How To Use Kanban to Deal With Issues 63

Using Key Performance Indicators 63

Avoiding Overproduction..68

Maintaining A Culture of Communication..............70

Ensuring Quality 74

Providing Excellent Customer Service.....................75

Chapter 6. Using Visualization Tools To Lead Your People To Success..............................79

Using the Kanban method 79

Implementing Lean Thinking 81

Maintaining an Agile environment 86

Applying the Scrum Framework 88

Chapter 7. How To Kanbanize Your Workplace And Develop Your Employees .. 91

Training For Managers 92

Fixing Skill Mismatch 93

Quality circles 94

Kaizen spirit 95

Use the PDCA technique 97

SMED 101

Standardized Work 101

Conclusion 106

Thank you 109

REFERENCES 110

Introduction

If you're looking to find a way to get maximum work efficiency, you're going to find a tool that can help you do exactly that through this book. This book will guide you on how to use Kanban and other work visualization tools in order to help you and your team boost your productivity.

It's a struggle to stay focused especially if the workload accumulates quicker than you can finish whatever you are currently handling. Not only that, it can become even more stressful when someone cannot finish the task they are working on because their skills do not match what they're doing, or that they're unmotivated.

Sometimes, it's the skills mismatch that causes the loss of motivation. When these things happen, expectations coming from the higher-ups and customers or clients are not met. Everyone becomes unhappy and the company loses resources. This is a far too common scenario.

I remember working with colleagues on several projects at once, thinking that multitasking helps finish the tasks at a faster pace. However, it became too stressful and somewhere in the middle of working those projects, the progress slowed down significantly and the quality of the output did not meet the demands of the clients. It cost us precious time, money, and potential clients since we were not able to accommodate new projects since we were still working on some projects.

There were also cases in which I worked on team projects, where each of the members is assigned specific tasks, and that the progress and results of each task are dependent on each other. Working on team projects required each and everyone in the team to have a full grasp of the progress of every aspect of the project. It was difficult especially since it's not easy to point out problems in the project due to everyone being busy on their specific tasks. It led to problems occurring later on during the project duration and it was too late to do something about the problems.

That's why I developed this book. I want you to know that there are tools out there that you can use.

With this book, you will be given techniques on effective visualization of the work. Not only that, but this book will also provide ideas on how to achieve the ideal output and work efficiency you're aiming for.

What Is Work Visualization?

Work visualization is simply the practice in which all aspects of work and workflow information is presented in visual form, hence the name. It involves presenting this information to all team members, managers, and stakeholders so that they can consume and process information quickly, and use it to be reminded of what needs to be done, who needs to do it, and where the team is in terms of progress.

Work visualization practice is a relatively modern practice. Traditionally, information about project status and direction cannot be easily accessed. People had their reports, project plans, and PowerPoint slides in their own desks and file cabinets. You had to request data from individual members manually, which takes time. In addition, some of the information is bound to be outdated. With work visualization, a more transparent manner of working is made possible.

Work visualization helps everyone in the company to see, know, and learn together. It is a simple and creative way of solving problems that can be used at every level of the organization. They enable everyone to see the differences between what was planned and what happened. Everyone can then help in finding root causes and developing countermeasures. It encourages people to work together on the problems and develop accountability towards achieving objectives without being overburdened.

Kanban is a work visualization technique that is aligned with Lean Thinking and Agile principles. Lean thinking, after all, is all about elimination of wastes, and Kanban is one tool that will highlight all the processes that produce waste. Agile methodologies, which Kanban falls under, focuses on maintaining quality and standards and controlling the total costs involved in the production of a particular product while meeting the demands of the customers. It goes with the idea that the demands coming from the customers should be met effectively at a rapid pace. And in this book, you'll learn about how to use these tools for your business.

Kanban in Action

Kanban is a scheduling system being used in just-in-time manufacturing and lean manufacturing in Japan. It works by enabling you to spot areas having problems through performance indicators such as cycle time and lead time. This approach is so effective that several companies from all over the world such as Spotify, Auto Trader (UK), Pixar, Zara, and DJ Orthopedics have been known to us it.

Mattias Jansson, working as an operations engineer at Spotify shared that the main problem in their operations was scalability. The operations team just cannot keep up with the needs and demands of the company. By implementing Kanban as the workflow management tool, lead times became shorter, many internal tasks are completed, and the departments the teams work with became happier with the performance.

Auto Trader, a company based in Manchester, UK decided to use Kanban to their advantage when they realized that many of the issues they've been facing are brought by various teams (e.g. Sysadmins, Release Team, Service Desk) working against each other. Prior to using Kanban, the email system the company was using has been contributing to the lack of teamwork, and to make up for the inefficiencies and difficulties in prioritizing, employees had to work a grueling 70 hours a week.

Ed Catmull, the president of Pixar, has recognized the need for Kanban in film production. A finished movie is basically an organized sequence of events. To complete the projects, each team transfers the idea to the next team, until the idea is pushed deeper into the chain. Through using Kanban boards, everyone working on a project has an idea of what the others are working on and everyone has an idea as to how their work can affect the works of the other members.

Kanban systems are applied to the store level at Zara. The store managers are given the responsibility to determine what, when, and how much of a product will be produced. Data on what the loyal customers demand are the basis of the orders they send to the headquarters twice a week.

Hospitals can also benefit the use of Kanban. Seattle Children's Hospital, for example, has been experiencing shortages in various items such as surgical dressings, clamps, catheters, and specialized tubing. This led to the nurses having to stockpile the goods at random locations in the hospital to make sure that they have the necessary items whenever the situation calls for it. Unfortunately, this non-standardized way of inventory storing led to work delays, which reduced the time that can be allotted to treat patients. When Kanban was implemented, a designated storage area was established, and information is collected and this database is maintained so that supplies are available when needed and the amount of expired goods is minimized. When they do expire, they are disposed of quickly. As a result, medical practitioners are given more time to deal and treat their patients.

Sustainability is one of the hallmarks of Kanban and Lean thinking, and one of the companies who have been integrating this principle into their manufacturing process is Nike.

Kimberley-Clark Corporation, makers of Kleenex, worked with Unipart on enhanced staff development and engagement, which lead to a reduction of staff absenteeism and better staff morale.

John Deere, 2003 world's biggest agricultural machinery manufacturer, spent $100 million in transforming its Iowa, U.S. operation to lean manufacturing which led to employees being able to identify and eliminate non-value-added activities wherever possible.

Companies working following the agile approach have a large network of suppliers and related companies that aid them in delivering products of high quality, which also gives them the advantages of being able to increase production as the consumer demand increases while also being able to redesign the products with issues from consumers.

By implementing Agile, 3M gained the ability to create self-organized teams which are also reactive to customer requirements and also were able to push forward priorities that they seem fit.

ANZ, a banking company based in Australia, now has the capability of releasing new functions on their banking application as needed, and has enjoyed massive recognition as a result.

Google, by applying customer feedback to their improvements basing on Agile, allows users to participate in Beta testings, which help identify bugs, major issues, and reports needed to apply to further update their products.

Spotify applied an agile environment by organizing its employees into squads. As the agile scrum method emphasizes on dividing work into chunks, Spotify used that principle by assigning each squad different tasks at hand. Results from that make Spotify one of the leading music streaming services globally.

Applying these techniques to your business will help you achieve success. There's nothing to lose and everything to gain when you gain an understanding of these techniques.

Many companies that have started implementing these techniques in their companies and reaped success afterward. You can get in on the action by reading this book.

Thanks for purchasing this book, I hope you enjoy it!

Chapter 1. Kanban As A Way to Visualize Work and Maximize Efficiency and Output

"One who conquers the sea today is ready to conquer the ocean tomorrow." -

Matshona Dhliwayo

All successful companies out there started small, but they triumphed over adversities to become what they are today. Many of these companies out there which are experiencing tremendous success have at one point also suffered from disorganization, lack of efficiency from working processes, work delays, lack of teamwork, and a whole host of other problems. At one point, their managers or founders thought twice as to whether they will be successful one day.

The only difference is that they never quit. Instead, they started to look for ways to make things better. They looked up ways to fine tune processes. They used techniques to pinpoint bottlenecks easily.

All processes and various tasks in a company can be visualized at a micro and macro level. Being able to oversee every corner of the tasks helps not only the company be more successful and gain more profit, but it can also improve and maximize the potentials and capabilities of every employee in the company. By having the capability to identify issues that hinder progress from work, it saves the company a lot of time, energy, and resources.

Kanban originally served as a scheduling system from the Toyota Production System, developed by Taiichi Ohno who at the time was an industrial engineer tasked to improve manufacturing efficiency. However, by the start of the 21st century, Kanban was introduced to other sectors and is now utilized in the software industry, through commercial sectors such as IT, software development, and marketing.

Kanban Cards

The word is a literal translation of the term "visual card." This is the defining feature of this tool; it makes use of Kanban cards, which are a visual representation of a particular task or work item. For example, a Kanban card can say something like "Fix reported bug on attachments." Some cards can be so detailed as to include a detailed list of tasks that need to be performed related to the work item as well as performance metrics. These cards are laid out on a Kanban board.

The Kanban approach works as a pull system, wherein production depends on the demands by the consumers, instead of a push system wherein services and products are offered towards the markets.

To maximize process efficiency and achieve the output goal, you should always make sure the process goes smoothly. To do that, you should be able to monitor the progress of the workflow from start to finish. Kanban works perfectly for that. One of the main reasons Kanban is being used by several companies is that it helps them easily visualize and track the workflow.

Kanban Columns

The simplest Kanban board includes three columns - requests, ongoing, finished. Once kanban cards are made, placed, and monitored, employees then will able to visualize the workflow and progress at a macro level, giving them the idea which work should be prioritized and which work should be done at a later date. With the Kanban board at the place, employees are also able to identify causes for work delays and prevent loopholes and issues that may arise.

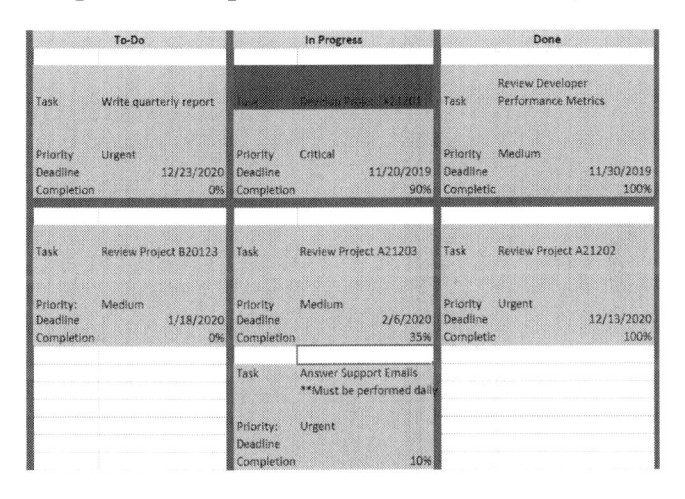

To-Do	In Progress	Done
Task: Write quarterly report	Task: Review Project A21201	Task: Review Developer Performance Metrics
Priority: Urgent Deadline: 12/23/2020 Completion: 0%	Priority: Critical Deadline: 11/20/2019 Completion: 90%	Priority: Medium Deadline: 11/30/2019 Completion: 100%
Task: Review Project B20123	Task: Review Project A21203	Task: Review Project A21202
Priority: Medium Deadline: 1/18/2020 Completion: 0%	Priority: Medium Deadline: 2/6/2020 Completion: 35%	Priority: Urgent Deadline: 12/13/2020 Completion: 100%
	Task: Answer Support Emails **Must be performed daily Priority: Urgent Deadline: Completion: 10%	

Example of a Kanban board

Kanban

Before the use of Kanban, many companies were not able to complete projects on time due to issues on prioritization. Back then, companies resorted to multitasking without placing a limit on how many works in progress should be addressed. However, contrary to popular belief, multitasking can do more harm than good.

So much time is lost when a team member loses focus due to context switching. In computing, context switching refers to the system of storing the state of a computer process so that it can be easily retrieved when needed and executed at the same point at which it was ended. It allows Central Processing Units to multitask. In humans, context switching refers to the process of switching from one task to the other, requiring mental effort to get to the state you were before you were interrupted. And it comes with a hidden cost. This is because it usually takes a while before you can gather your bearings and focus on the task at hand after your attention was diverted from it either by another task or a simple distraction such as your phone ringing or a colleague gossiping.

Sure, a team can focus on several tasks by optimizing what each one should be doing and when, and a team member certainly can work on multiple tasks; however, there should be a limit on how many tasks should be completed within a designated period. Employees are human too and having too many tasks to handle at once reduces the amount of attention they can give to each task, which causes them to work inefficiently and ultimately lead to project delays.

Kanban helps you visualize the projects you handle in an organized manner through the use of a Kanban board and Kanban cards. With the use of the Kanban board, you can help your employees organize the tasks they need to do for the day. It also helps them track the progress of the projects assigned to them, and determine which project to prioritize. Additionally, it helps them work efficiently since the overall workflow is monitored, making sure that causes for delays and other issues are pointed out and dealt with as soon as it is identified.

WIP (Work In Progress) Limits

With Kanban, the amount of work in progress is limited in all parts of the workflow. By setting the maximum amount of items per given stage, it is guaranteed that another task will only be dealt with once there's an available slot, making sure that the employees can focus on and work efficiently at the tasks they are handling at the moment. And because there are limits, you would need to evaluate which tasks are a priority. You will also be able to highlight problems in the workflow so you can resolve them.

To ensure production flows smoothly, you should always monitor the overall work progress. The use of visualization tools such as Kanban methodology makes monitoring the overall progress of the tasks a lot easier.

To make sure that the process works smoothly, overproduction should be avoided at all times. Kanban prevents overproduction by controlling the production rate using the demand rate. With one of its goals being prevention of excess inventory, a limit is placed at the start of the process based on the number of items waiting to be delivered at supply points.

Additionally, the inability to forecast demands from consumers causes vital problems in the production. It can lead to either producing over or less than what is being demanded by consumers. Kanban is utilized in this situation as a way to trigger demand signal that is immediately forwarded to the supply chain, so the supply chain responds to the demands required by the consumers. With that, there is the assurance that the inventory held in the supply chain is managed better and that they can deliver the demands of the consumers at the right pace.

The use of the Kanban gives your employees the ability to visualize the overall workflow and the ability to point out hindrances in the progression of the workflow.

Chapter 2: Lean Thinking

Lean thinking is a practice that promotes the idea that we should always on the lookout for things that can provide more benefit and value to society and individuals while reducing if not outright removing wastes.

Kanban is a fundamental practice in lean thinking because it allows you to identify where waste occurs in the workflow to prevent further unnecessary costs and use of resources. It enables employees to be aware of which projects need to be done right away while avoiding overproduction. Implementing Kanban is a great way to practice lean thinking, empowering employees to meet changes in market behavior.

The term was coined by Daniel T. Jones and James P. Womack as a representation for the insights they gained in-depth analysis of the Toyota Production System.

Toyota's way of training their managers throughout the years focused on developing its employees' abilities of reasoning instead of pushing them to follow systems developed by specialists. The company also has a group of elders and coordinators who are dedicated to aiding and teaching their managers on how to think differently and how to do better at their job by focusing on core aspects:

The Workplace

Focusing on the workplace entails making regular visits to the place where specific tasks take place. Being in the place and experiencing firsthand what happens there gives the managers and other employees the idea of what happens there. This also enables management to get a bird's eye view of the project. As a result, they acquire the capability to assess the works in progress and determine if there is rooms for improvement.

Additionally, being present also gives the employees an avenue to express their concerns regarding the work in progress and other things to the management. These concerns being addressed gives the impression to the employees that they have support and respect from the management.

Visiting the workplace and engaging your people leaves them the impression that you genuinely care, value and trust them. This also boosts morale, as it gives employees more confidence. Having confident and dedicated employees is good for your business.

Value

The Lean approach begins with a detailed understanding of what value the customer assigns to product and services. This is what determines what the customer will pay. Establishing value allows organizations to create a top-down target price. The cost to produce the products and services is then determined. The organization focuses on eliminating waste so that they can deliver the value the customer expects at the highest level of profitability.

Value refers to what a customer is willing to pay to acquire certain products or services. For a business to be profitable, it must create something of value at the least amount of cost. This requires a two-pronged approach. First, you must get an understanding of your customers. That way, you can create something that they would deem useful. You need to implement a system that would help prevent production and delivery of defective work. This is a way to prevent the likelihood of customers spending money on your products and being dissatisfied with them. Lean management practitioners refer to this practice as building value through built-in quality is tied to this.

Next, you should remove as much waste as possible. Make sure that you are conserving the company's effort, time, energy, and resources. This means putting a stop to something in the process once you see there is something wrong or doubtful in the process of the item being produced.

Value streams

A value stream refers to the entirety of the product's life cycle, which spans the collection of raw materials, the period in which the finished product is in use, and ultimately, the disposal of the product. This means that you'll need a good understanding of your "takt" time. Note that in management systems such as Lean, Takt time refers to the rate at which a production team should complete a product in order to meet demand. The takt time rhythm results in the creation of stable value streams in which the stable teams are tasked to work on stable sets of products with given stable equipment instead of optimizing the usage of specified machines or processes.

Lean thinking must be practiced to study this stream in detail. All processes must be examined to verify if it adds value to the product. Anything that does not contribute, be it steps, materials, or product features, must be reviewed. Note that any part of the value stream can be either of this three:

- Will clearly create value

- Will not create value but the waste is unavoidable due to the current technology
- Will not create value and is easily and immediately avoidable

Flow

Another aspect essential to the elimination of waste in the process is the complete understanding of the flow of processes. If the stream seems to have stalled at a certain point, that means waste will be or has been produced. Sometimes, that is unavoidable. It can, however be reduced, as highlighted in the previous section on waste by developing a value chain where each process is full in step with all the others.

Unfortunately, almost all traditional businesses are addicted to batch processes, wherein processes are aimed to produce as many items are possible with the goal of reducing the unit costs to a minimum value. Lean thinking approaches the matter in another way, wherein the focus is on the optimization of the workflow that the general cost of the business is reduced at a dramatic rate through the elimination of the need for transportation, subcontractor usage, systems, and warehouses.

Pull

Lean thinking has the goal of ensuring that every step in the process is executed because it is needed at a precise point in time. No step will be performed well ahead of time, preventing buildup of WIP inventory and bottlenecks. Synchronized flow will be maintained as a result. Rather than using the traditional American manufacturing approach of pushing work through based on a forecast and schedule, the pull approach dictates that nothing is made until there is demand for it.

This means that decision makers need to envision the differences between ideal and actual scenarios at any time in the workplace. This is where the use of visualization tools such as Kanban cards boards will be handy. With such a board, you can pull work from upstream depending on what you takt time dictates.

Additionally, it also requires efficient ways of voicing what is required in each step in the value chain. Sure, there is tension created because having a pull system requires flexibility and short design-to-delivery cycle periods. Nonetheless, pulling will enable the team to edge closer to single-piece-work. The team can identify issues as they show up, which can lead to the prevention of bigger problems. This can also contribute to complex situations being solved over time.

Excellence

Lastly, lean thinking is about instilling the kaizen spirit in every employee in your company. Kaizen refers to the notion of changing for the better albeit in small and sustainable ways. The kaizen spirit means looking for the 1% change for a hundred times from every team member instead of an instantaneous 100% change. Through the practice of kaizen, self and the collective confidence to face larger challenges is developed.

The ultimate goal of lean thinking is not to the application of the tools to all processes, but by seeking perfection by changing for the better. Smart systems or go-it-alone people are not the main contributors to perfection and are not sought after. It is the dedication from everyone in the company to improve things hand-with-hand little by little that matters. By applying lean thinking in the overall workflow, the monitoring and reduction of wastes will be ensured.

Chapter 3. Agile And Scrum

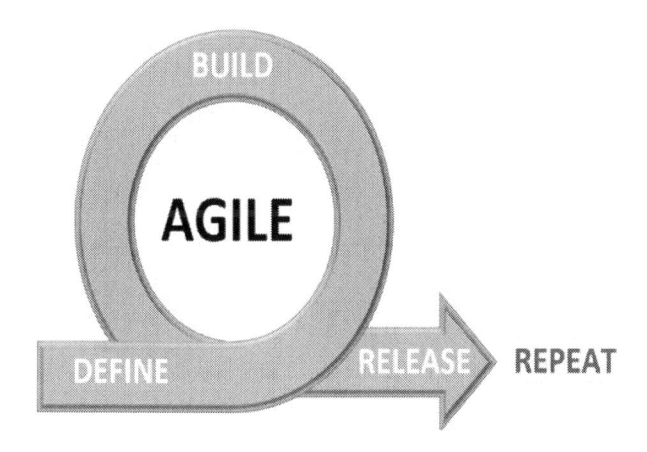

Agile is a compilation of methodologies focusing on the concept of iterative development, in which the requirements and solutions evolve or change by collaborating with teams capable of self-organization and are cross-functional. This management technique is often used in software development.

The advantages of Agile development are numerous. These include:

- giving the teams the capability to provide value
- having greater predictability,
- greater quality,

- greater skills to react to changes in demands from consumers, and
- faster delivery.

The most used agile methodologies are Kanban and Scrumban (Which is a hybrid of Kanban and Scrum). That's why this book will also cover Scrum and Agile.

The Benefits Of Going Agile

An advantage of an agile environment is that it promotes and develops teams to be self-organizing and accountable. Self-organization promotes initiative from employees and teaches employees to multitask while maintaining things in order. Being accountable means employees and teams recognize their responsibilities with the tasks appointed to them, that they can deliver what is asked of them, and if they are not able to do so, they can justify their actions and mishaps.

In an agile environment, engineering practices that are aimed to deliver high-quality items at a rapid pace is present. With these practices being employed throughout the processes, there's an assurance that consumer demands and expectations are met as fast as possible. This results to a great customer experience, and the positive impression increasing the likelihood that customers or clients will keep coming back.

The agile way of approaching business aligns the development of the products made corresponding with the demands from consumers and the goals of the company.

The 12 Principles

The modern Agile process is derived from the Agile Manifesto, which was developed by seventeen experts in software development. The manifesto presented the twelve principles that business should abide by if they want to improve their processes.

1. The highest priority should be satisfaction of the consumers, which can be achieved by punctual and continuous delivery of valuable software.

2. Be open to change. Accept changing requirements, even when they appear at

the later parts of development. Agile processes should be able to help customers gain a competitive advantage.

3. Frequently deliver working software, and the preferred timescale should be as short as possible.

4. Developers and business people should work together daily for the whole duration of the project.

5. Continuously give the individuals in the team motivation, support, and trust that they can finish their tasks at the given timescale.

6. Keep in mind that face-to-face conversation has consistently proven to be the most effective and efficient means of discussing information to and with the team.

7. The primary measure of progress of the work-in-progress is working software. If you can develop prototypes, that's well and good, but you need to present something that actually works, rough

edges and all, to be able to say that there's progress.

8. Sustainability is importance. Everyone involved including developers and users should be able to maintain a constant pace. The beauty of agile development is that the short bursts of activity keeps morale high. Burnout may happen but if you keep workloads at manageable levels, team members should be able to cope. However, if you bite off way more than you can chew, your team's motivation would be impaired.

9. To be able to enhance the agility of the processes, attention to good design and technical excellence should be maintained.

10. It is essential to have simplicity in the works, to maximize the amount of work not done.

11. It is from the teams that can self-organize that the best designs, architectures, and requirements spring from. This means

that managers should be wary of micromanaging. The best course of action is to develop a team that can be trusted, and to foster that trust.

12. Twelfth, teams should reflect on how to be more effective, then adjust all behaviors corresponding from the reflections, all of that at regular intervals.

Incorporating all the twelve principles of the agile manifesto in your agile environment will not only aid ease the work processes, but also it will mold and develop the work ethic and dedication of the employees in the company. Having an effective and efficient work process plus dedicated employees will surely give the company the advantage.

The incorporation of the twelve principles of the agile manifesto in your agile environment makes the work a lot easier. It also allows everyone in the business holistically to develop themselves. Embodying the principles daily will improve the efficiency of the work and maximizes the quality of the product being made.

Customer demands change through time and employees find it difficult to deal with these. In an agile environment, however, accepting changes in requirements given by the consumers at an earlier or later notice is encouraged. Through the second principle of the Agile Manifesto, everyone is trained and developed to be able to adapt to the ever-changing customer demands.

Missing the deadline before getting the work done is a common problem in business for a long time ago. However, everyone can be trained to work quickly and efficiently through an agile environment. With the agile manifesto's third principle, employees are trained to deliver the required projects in the shortest amount of time possible.

There are occasions that the people working on a project are not able to agree with each other on the specifics in the project. This causes work delays and low product quality. To prevent issues, the fourth principle of the agile manifesto requires everyone involved in the project to work on it together daily for the whole duration of the product development.

It is unfortunate that sometimes, employees are not able to deliver their full potential to the projects given to them. Sometimes, tasks given to the employees are too simple, perhaps due to them being new to the company, leading to a waste of potential. These things can be fixed with the sixth principle of the agile manifesto, wherein every member of the team is given motivation and support.

Miscommunication can be a hindrance in workflow. The sixth principle suggests that a face-to-face conversation is the most efficient and effective way of discussing information with the whole team, wherein by having it regularly assures that no information is left not discussed.

In a project, an assurance that there is positive progress is the presence of a product that meets the quality demanded by its consumers. Without a product to show to investors or stakeholders, the support provided by these people might just be withdrawn from your company. Through the agile manifesto's seventh principle, everyone working in the project is required to deliver a product that satisfies the quality demands of the consumers.

The quality of the product is vital to the customers who will use it. Customers will choose your product when you can meet their expectations. The continuous giving of attention to technical excellence and good design, which what the ninth principle of the agile manifesto promotes, guarantee that the products you produce are at the optimum quality.

Extra attention to detail even though it is not required is an example of muda in lean thinking, referred to as over-processing. By applying simplicity to your work, which is through only doing work which is necessary to the overall workflow, maximizes the capability and time that can be allotted to projects that are yet to be done.

In an agile environment, teams are trained to be able to self-organize. They can decide on things and do their tasks without the frequent guidance and supervision of the management. With that, an environment build in trust exists. As what the eleventh principle of the agile manifesto pronounce, the best requirements, designs, and architectures come from teams who are cable of self-organization.

Like the concept of kaizen in lean thinking, the twelfth principle in agile manifesto promotes regular reflection on improving the employees' effectiveness and adjusting their behaviors in accordance to their reflections. By doing so, the employees are allowed to further enhance their skills and capabilities in their respective jobs. Everyone's improvement guarantees a greater overall workflow efficiency and maximization of the product quality.

Scrum

Scrum is a lightweight process framework and one of the many used in agile development. It is also the most preferred by many companies.

Process frameworks are sets of practices that should be followed to ensure consistency. Being lightweight means that the running costs of the processes are kept at the minimum as much as possible to maximize the amount of productive time that is available for getting valuable work done.

Scrum is often used in managing complex software and product development. It makes use of incremental and iterative practices, giving organizations the ability to adjust to rapid-changing requirements while producing products that meet the developing goals of the business.

A basic Scrum team consists of three members, the Product Owner, the Development Team, and the ScrumMaster. Each of these members has their specific roles in a project. In an agile environment that uses the Scrum framework, a scrum team is expected to be cross-functional and self-organizing.

Unfortunately, in some companies, teams are reliant on the management for the work that needs to be done. They only follow the orders of their higher-ups on the tasks that need to be taken care of. With the capability to self-organize, teams are allowed to choose which approach works best for them to get the task done at the projected deadline.

Kanban

There are also cases that the teams ask outside help just to get things done. This comes with risks because there is no assurance that outside help provides a positive effect on the task that needs to be completed. Being cross-functional, teams are expected to have the capability to accomplish the task at hand without relying on outside help. With that, teams are trained to optimize their creativity, flexibility, and productivity.

Scrum teams carry out projects through iteration and increments, making sure that all factors coming from the feedback of the consumers are addressed. Through increment deliveries of the finished product, it guarantees that a tangible product is always available for use.

The implementation of the Scrum framework in an agile environment gives you the advantage of increasing the quality of the items to be delivered. In an agile environment, it is necessary to deliver the working product frequently and at intervals with short timescales. As a result, there will be an assurance that the product you will end up completing will be of high quality. This is because in an agile environment, products are regularly checked and changed based on the consumers' feedback.

The scrum framework also helps teams adjust and keep up with changes due to the access to certain information such as consumer feedback and demands regarding the products. Not only that, the framework is built in such a way that change is expected, which is a hallmark of agile development. In a software development setting, accepting the changes and working to address changing demands gives your clients a huge competitive advantage. The products you develop for customers will leave a good impression about the company and the teams behind it, and this could lead to more sales and profits.

Another advantage when using the Scrum framework is the ability make more accurate predictions, especially as regards consumer demands, meanwhile also spending less creating the products with the corresponding consumer demands. Having better estimates enables your organization to save a lot of time, effort, energy, and resources. As a result, you may redirect these resources toward other projects or endeavors that can generate value.

The defining characteristic of scrum is the ability to control the schedule and state of the projects. It gives you the idea as to which project needs prioritization and which projects can wait for a little longer. It also enables you to point out issues and bottlenecks in the workflow.

Maintaining an agile environment gives an assurance that the quality is met because regular inspections and developments are done, at a short time scale. For projects and tasks which include fast-paced changes through time, iterative development works better. An agile environment applying the Scrum framework makes it a lot easier to deal with feedback and demand from consumers which come at a rapid pace.

Kanban and other work visualization tools allow you to pinpoint problems earlier on so that efficiency is maintained. The following chapter is about how neglecting the issues in your company, be it in your employees, the management, the process flow, or equipment can bring you a lot more problems later on.

Knowing how important it is to address the problems in your company will give you insights on how you can improve performance from the individual to the organizational level.

Chapter 4. Why An Organization Needs Kanban: Overlooked Issues That May Cause Massive Problems

Kanban, as one of the Agile methodologies, has been developed with the ultimate goal of improving performance by giving an entire team a bird's eye view of what needs to be done, when it needs to be done, and who needs to do it. The beauty of Kanban is that it allows managers to see their team's capabilities and empowers every person in the team by setting limits, thereby encouraging sustainability.

Without tools such as Kanban, two things can happen: tasks will not be completed on time, leading to delays, or the team could fall victim to overwork, leading to burnout.

As Colin Powell said, "Never neglect details. When everyone's mind is dulled or distracted, the leader must be doubly vigilant."

Every aspect of the business should be checked regularly. Additionally, there are moments that the team is fixated on the tasks at their hand that they are not able to assess the bigger picture, wherein you can see it, so you must do something about it.

An essential part of a growing business is handling issues, whether they come from the consumers of the product or services being offered by the business, or from the team, the workflow, or the management. Being made aware of these issues allows you to make improvements on the products and services you offer. Neglecting these issues and being complacent will bring bigger problems, the worst of them being bankruptcy.

Poor management

One of the many problems being faced by businesses is the lack of Key Performance Indicators and the lack of monitoring of these indicators. These indicators provide criteria that give insights as to whether within the business, or a certain aspects of operation, is going well or taking a bad turn.

Neglecting these indicators will bring a lot of problems which include overproduction, lack of efficiency in the workflow, and work delays.

Overproduction is a common problem in businesses which occurs when companies are producing items more than what is demanded by the consumers. Failure to address this problem costs a lot, including money, energy, resources, and time. Companies that apply the push system are usually the ones who encounter this problem.

Another problem faced by companies is neglecting the reject ratio. This ratio measures the waste that was produced during the production of an item. Early on, a threshold should be set and alarm bells should ring if the amount of scrap that is being rejected is well below or above the ratio. After all, the goal of lean management techniques such as Kanban is to minimize waste in order to be more profitable. The reject ratio should be within acceptable limits.

However, a reject ratio that is too low might be an indicator of a lax quality assurance process, which could lead to customer satisfaction problems. Therefore, managers should constantly monitor these aspects.

Balancing production and the quality of work done by the employees is a headache if not managed properly. Growing companies tend to neglect one of the two while focusing on the other, which leads to several other problems later on. These problems include inefficiency, backlogs, low quality work offered, and the inability to keep up with the ever-changing customer demands in the market.

A study conducted on communication by the Society for HR Management includes four hundred companies with a hundred thousand employees each shows that lack of proper communication causes a loss of $62.4 million in average due to misaligned work, overhead, incorrect deliverables, and a lot more. The continuous lack of proper means of communication between all people in the company, not only a great amount of money will be lost, but also may lead to other worse problems, and eventually, bankruptcy.

Contributing factors to lack of proper communication include vague requirements, lack of enough experience, the fear of disappointment from the management's end, which may eventually lead to fear of losing one's job, poor processes and ego. Not establishing proper channels of communication may be detrimental to the growth and success of the company. It may also cause internal disputes between the employees and the management.

Retaining customers is also one of the many struggles in business. Businesses may lose customers if there is a decrease in product quality, a price increase of the product, and inability to meet the consumers' expected deadlines. Without customers, it will not be possible for companies to earn profit especially if there is intense competition.

Problems with employees

Motivating employees is a tough challenge, be it for startups or large corporations. On average, demotivated employees in startup businesses contribute about twenty percent of the total manpower. Not dealing with these employees may eventually lead to the bankruptcy of startup businesses.

For the case of large corporations, neglecting to motivate employees may lead to them providing only the bare minimum of effort, energy, and dedication at their tasks, having in mind that they work only to stay employed. These may lead to several problems, which include little to no quality provided at the work done, delays in the progress of the tasks at hand, missed deadlines, and absenteeism.

The presence of these problems will be costly for corporations as it may result to not being able to open up branches, extensions, or another business. The worst scenario is bankruptcy.

It is also a struggle for companies to train employees of the older generation with the new technologies present in society. Training is an expensive investment since it may take weeks, months or a year to make sure that the employees are properly oriented on how new technologies work. With that, companies may suffer overhead in operations, and eventually in the overall workflow.

Lack of proper utilization of employees is also a common struggle for different businesses worldwide. A mismatch between the employee's skills and the tasks assigned to that employee leads to work delays and low-quality work provided by the employee. Another example is not maximizing the potential of each employee in the company, which also leads to low quality work is given and work delays.

Iceberg of Ignorance

Sidney Yshido conducted a study dated 1989. The research showed that in many organizations, there is a disconnect among senior-level management. Many senior level managers seem to be unable to comprehend the processes and systems which can affect both the employees and the customers.

The iceberg of ignorance is in reference to this phenomenon in which senior level managers are aware of only 4% of the existing problems.

Middle managers are aware of approximately 9%, with supervisors being aware of 74%, and the front-liners being aware of 100%. These are just rough numeral representations. The exact number may actually vary.

The most troubling thing from this study is that the people who are responsible and can solve the problems are the ones who don't even have the slightest idea of the problems that exist for the front-line employees, who are the ones responsible for serving the customers.

The executive-level leadership in the company must be aware of the problems that exist in the company, be it faulty equipment, an outdated computer software, or a broken process. These people should be aware of them to be able to help provide positive change for the employees and ultimately the consumers.

With a Kanban board maintained at various levels including the organizational level and front-line operations, individuals and management at every level can have a better look at how the business is doing.

Poor Customer Service

Customer service is another problem commonly encountered in all businesses. Multiple occasions of bad customer service will leave the consumers a bad image towards the company, which is detrimental to the growth and success of the company. The worst-case scenario will be shutting down the business.

No matter how good your products are, if you are not able to meet the consumers' expectations of your services, consumers will still not be satisfied with what is offered to them. If your customer service is not satisfactory for these customers, you will not have them as returning customers.

If you don't take the concerns, complaints, and feedback of consumers on your or your employees' performance, you will not be able to monitor progress. You will not be able to take action to rectify problems in a timely manner. This will only result to a negative impact on the reputation of the business.

With the presence of social media platforms such as Facebook, Twitter, Google Plus, Instagram, and a lot more, unsatisfied consumers will not hesitate to use these platforms to voice out their concerns and complaints that you have neglected. Negative comments posted on these platforms spread out at a rapid pace worldwide, resulting to massive damage on your brand's reputation.

Despite how established the business is, a bad reputation due to terrible customer services will leave a negative impact that will surely affect the business. Repeat customers, sales, and feedback from customers affect the growth and survival of your company. Poor customer service will result to a decrease in customer loyalty, brand value, and ultimately profits.

Muda

Waste reduction is one of the vital goals in lean thinking that is practiced to increase profitability. Muda, mura, and muri are the three types of deviation from the optimal allocation of resources which must be eliminated in order to increase profits.

Mura refers to inconsitence. With Kanban entailing a pull process, variation will be apparent. The sizes and types of requirements may vary on each iteration. Sometimes, variation cannot be avoided and is even encourages, such as in the case of design options being used to innovate. There is, however, variation that can be quickly avoided such as the use of various tools instead of a standard one, or adhering to different standards instead of establishing a universal set of standards.

Muri refers to overburden and this is in fact what must be dealt with first. This harks back to the principle of sustainability that Agile development promotes. Burnout must be prevented. If individuals and entire teams are overwhelmed, waste is likely to occur in the long run. Crazy work hours should be the exception, not the norm. This is why Kanban makes use of WIP limits, which sets a realistic workload for a specific iteration. With these limits, backlog is prevented, customers are satisfied, and the team would feel empowered that they are able to deliver.

In lean management, muda is typically used interchangeably with "waste." So it's the term that is often used whenever lean thinking principles are discussed. Its literal translation is wastefulness or futility. It is any hindrance that causes waste to be present in the production.

Taiichi Ohno, known as the father of the Toyota Production System, has seven hindrances or Muda identified, wherein when these hindrances are neglected, lessens the profits that can be earned by the company. These hindrances are transport, motion, waiting, inventory, over-processing, overproduction, and defects. An eighth Muda, termed as unused skill or talent, is later identified since dealing with this waste is a key factor in dealing with the original seven.

1. Transport, the first hindance, is the movement of products even though it is not necessary to be done in the course of the overall process. By moving the products, it is exposed to risks of being damaged, delayed, or lost. Transporting products unnecessarily does not add

anything to the value of the product and consumers are not willing to pay for that.

2. Motion, the second hindrance, is the unnecessary movement of the people or equipment during the creation of the product. It also covers the costs and damage inflicted on what creates the product. It includes repetitive strain injuries of the workers, wear and tear of the equipment, and unnecessary downtime.

3. If a product is not being processed or transported to a location, it is waiting. A large amount of time wasted is allotted to the waiting of the product to be worked on. Neglecting the increase in waiting time may lead to missing deadlines.

4. Inventory refers to all components, work in progress, and finished items that are yet to be processed. All of these represent a capital outlay which has yet to be converted to income. The longer the remain in the waiting stage, the more it

will be damaging to the overall process and also to the company's profits.

5. Over-processing refers to doing more than what is required by the consumers. It also includes using components which are more complex, more precise, higher in quality and more expensive than what is only required. By doing so, it results in the delay in the production of the item and the spiking at high levels of production costs.

6. Production in large batches often results in creating more of a product than what has demanded leads to several wastes. It should be noted that the needs of the consumers change regularly and it changes quicker than the time that is consumed in creating large batches of products. Overproduction is considered as the worst kind of waste that can occur in a business.

7. Defective works or components are either discarded or reworked to achieve the demanded quality by the consumers. Inspecting and fixing defects not only cost

effort, but also energy, time, and resources that should be allocated to other tasks. Defects result in additional delays and costs, which decreases the company's profits.

8. Unfortunately, there are circumstances wherein companies do not efficiently utilize their workers' skills, talents, and capabilities, which is also a waste. There are even situations that for knowledge to be not shared, workers are permitted to work in silos. Without taking into account the proper matching and utilization of the workers' skills miss companies the opportunities that lie with it.

You should take note of the issues your company is facing, whether you are an employee or you are an owner. Problems should be addressed as soon as you see them. The following chapter will talk about how dealing with the issues will provide growth and success to the company.

Chapter 5. Taking Control: How To Use Kanban to Deal With Issues

Neglecting your problems will only give you a lot more problems to deal with later on. In this chapter, we will be talking about the benefits of dealing with the issues in the company.

Problems, in a way, help businesses grow. You can continuously bring satisfaction to the consumers despite issues. Dealing with the issues bring growth to each and everyone in the company, resulting in better performances, higher profits, and ultimately, success.

Using Key Performance Indicators

Key Performance indicators give you insight as to how the performances in the business go.

Note that the KPIs that would be most beneficial for your monitoring efforts may vary depending on the kind of project you're working on. For example, for social media marketing projects, engagements e.g. likes, comments, and retweets would be a good KPI. If you're in website development, Average Lead Time is a good KPI.

Here's a list of KPIs that are likely to be useful for businesses engaged in digital technology and marketing:

- **Average Lead time**

    This refers to the time it takes you to transform an idea into an actual product. In some industries, this spans the time during which a prototype has been developed and is ready to be moved to production. In others, it refers to the span of time during which an idea is formed and a product that is ready for use is developed. However, it usually does not take into account the time an idea is left in the "waiting period." You can even classify the items to organize your data. You can set ALT per priority, or per project size, or per customer.

- **Queues**

    This refers to the list of items that are waiting to be processed, so they're supposed to be "waiting in between stages."

Let's say your Kanban board has a column for "For completion", another for "For Review" and another for "For delivery". Once a project has been completed, it will be moved to the For Review section. If too many projects get completed because there are many members taking care of that task, a queue might start to form in the "For Review section if the project reviewers cannot keep up. Now, project delivery typically requires minimal effort and can be quickly performed, so it's not likely that a queue will form in that section even if it's manned by just one person. Nonetheless, queues are an indicator of where the bottlenecks are.

- **Work in Progress (WIP)**

These refers to tasks that have been started but have yet to be finished. When you are able to track these tasks, you can help improve flow. Keep in mind that technically, all WIP do not add value to the customer. After all, customers won't be able to use unfinished work. You can only really consider the value when a project is completed and ready for the customer's use.

- **Reject Ratio**

    As mentioned, this measures the scrap that was produced during the production of an item, which spans the entire cycle. A threshold should be set earlier on and ideally, action should be taken if the reject ratio is too high.

- **Blockers**

    In Kanban, blocking refers to the art of marking an item as "frozen." These are the things that have completely stalled. This is different from items that are just waiting to be processed (i.e. those in a queue).

These are the items that are in limbo, awaiting an external dependency. For example, a client placed an order but part of the instructions is vague and requires clarification. Work is stalled until the client can provide clarifications.

- **Average Cycle Time**
  This refers to the amount of time it takes to complete a particular stage. So if a project requires multiple steps, the cycle time refers to the time it takes to complete one step. The time it takes for all the steps to be processed is the lead time. In Kanban, the goal is to optimize cycle time which means that you also have to consider the amount of work and resources that each step of the process requires. Be careful when optimizing cycle times because messing with one can result to dire consequences for another.

One of the indicators companies use is the reject ratio, wherein it measures the scrap that was

Kanban

produced during the production of an item. Through the Kanban method, monitoring of this indicator and other indicators will be easy since the by using a kanban board and kanban cards, you will be able to monitor the overall processes and the specifics of each part of the process.

By setting these indicators in your business, you will immediately know as to which part of the business needs changes or improvement. Every business, to be successful, places a handful of these indicators for them to know whether they made any progress at all and act accordingly depending on what these indicators show. Monitoring the overall workflow includes monitoring KPIs since these indicators will save you from problems that include overproduction, work delays, and lack of efficiency in the workflow.

Avoiding Overproduction

It's tempting to produce as many items you can during times wherein there is an idle equipment time or workers. However, by doing so, it does not do you any good and leads to a lot more problems later on which includes higher storage costs, work delays, product defects, higher capital expenditure, and excessive lead time. By eliminating overproduction, you can save a lot of money, time, resources, and energy that can be allocated to doing other tasks or projects.

Knowing as to how much product you should produce is essential and producing more than what is demanded will not do you good. By producing only what is required, you will be able to save a lot of time and resources which can be allocated to other tasks or products in the future. Avoiding overproduction is a must and you should never allow any instances of this in your business.

There are instances that scrap products are present in the production and there are a lot of factors that can attribute to that. Companies set reject ratios into the production of their products to regulate the production of scrap products. By following the established reject rations, companies can save resources, energy, and time which can later be used for other purposes.

Company growth and the quality of work done by the employees should go hand-in-hand. If you buy new equipment to improve your services, you should also train your staff to handle the new equipment efficiently. By doing so, you can be assured that the quality of services being offered to the customers is what you have perceived when you bought that new equipment for your business.

If it's the case wherein you bought new machinery for your factories or facilities having in mind that it will improve the rate of production of the items you sell, you should train your employees as to how to properly handle these types of equipment and you also need to make changes in the overall workflow. By doing so, you will be able to guarantee that the quality of the item being produced with the new equipment will be what the consumers are demanding.

Maintaining A Culture of Communication

Proper communication is necessary to assure that everything works fine in the business.

Setting up proper channels of communication, be it through meetings or regular check-ups of the facilities gives the avenue for both the workers and owners to express their concerns and ideas, which will be for the betterment of the business. It is also through these communications that owners and workers will have engagements with each other wherein owners can show their support and gratitude to workers which will surely give workers the morale boost they need to work hard.

Retention of loyal customers in business is hard nowadays due to the presence of competitors. Making sure that retain loyal customers is a must since these customers give you a stable profit. They also give you an avenue to attract potential customers due to good impressions which are brought by the positive feedback of these loyal customers.

Keeping Employees Motivated

Boosting your employees will not cost you anything. After all, these employees work their

Kanban

selves to their limits to meet not only your expectations but also the expectations of the customers. Boosting their morale can be through engaging with them regularly, or providing incentives after a job well done. Motivating your employees will ensure that they give their full dedication in achieving their tasks, which in turn will surely boost the company's sales.

If you are in a startup business, it is necessary to make sure that your colleagues are fully motivated at all times. Demotivated employees may take up around twenty percent of the manpower of the whole team, which surely when left demotivated will cause a big disaster in the overall progress of the work being done. Motivating your colleagues every once in a while will make sure that they are working at their full potential, making things easier for the whole team.

For cases of large corporations, demotivated employees only work at their bare minimum having in mind that they do things for them to be still employed in the company. If you're having colleagues that are not motivated, it will affect the progress of the work you're both in. By keeping them motivated, it will assure you that the tasks appointed to your team will be done on time.

If you're a team leader, a supervisor, or in any managerial position in the company and you have colleagues under you which are demotivated, it will give problems not only to the work assigned in your team but also to the company when these employees will be ignored. By boosting the morale of these employees in any way you can, you will be sure that the whole team will work efficiently and that deadlines will surely be met at an earlier time. With that, company operations will go smoothly and the company goals will surely be achieved.

Newer technologies lead to newer techniques and approaches on how to make a job done in the shortest time possible. Training your employees, especially of the older generation, on how to properly handle these new technologies can be a struggle at times, and may cost you a lot of time. Adjusting the work processes and introducing a new comprehensible workflow will ensure that there will be no delays in the work being done since every employee will be able to understand it.

Employers should also know the capabilities, talents, and skills of their employees and that these skills should be utilized in the right way. A good match between the employees' skills and the tasks provided will surely shorten the time it takes to get the job done. With that, resources and energy will be saved while there is no need for the quality of the work to suffer.

Ensuring Quality

Consumers demand high-quality products and by producing defective items, not only you don't meet their expectations, but they also cause you delays on work. By making sure that the quality of the products you produce are at the quality demanded by the consumers, you can save a lot of time and money.

Providing Excellent Customer Service

Consumers want excellent customer service from businesses. A bad experience will leave the consumers a bad impression of the company. Maintaining excellent customer service, on the other hand, leaves a good impression on the consumers. Chances are they will surely return to your company as loyal customers. Loyal customers provide companies a stable income.

Concerns, complaints, and feedback from consumers of your products or services should be handled. Kanban, being an Agile methodology, enables you to take this further by enabling your company to meet changing customer demands.

Happy customers will spread the word of their experience to other people. With the presence of social media platforms such as Facebook, Twitter, and Google Plus, these happy consumers will not think twice of talking about their experience. Positive comments posted on these platforms spread out at a rapid pace worldwide, not only leaving your company a good reputation but also attracting potential customers.

Kanban

Keeping a good reputation through excellent customer service can contribute to greater profits. Not only that, but it can be an avenue also for potential investors and business partners to open offers to your business.

Waste Elimination

By minimizing transport, or the unnecessary movement of products and people in the duration of the process, it prevents products from being exposed to damage and defects. It also prevents unnecessary workload, wears, and tears of equipment, and exhaustion of employees. Transport does not affect the value of the product and its elimination will prevent unnecessary expenses for the company.

Elimination of motion, or the movement of the people or equipment during production when it is unnecessary to do so, will save you a lot of time that can be allotted to do other tasks. By making sure that you have a well-organized workspace, the equipment that you will use is placed near the location of the production, and that the materials you need are placed in an ergonomic position, you will not only save excess time that you might use for a motion, you will also save energy.

Eliminating waiting time can make the work needed to be done at a shorter time scale. With having the work done at a quicker pace, another work that needs to be done can be worked out sooner. It also prevents excess inventory since raw materials will be used before it degrades and it also prevents overproduction since there will be no excess inventory.

Buying raw materials only when it is required and only in the required quantities will eliminate excess inventory. By its elimination, additional expenses, inefficient use of energy and resources, and work delays can be prevented. The materials that are conserved with its elimination can be used in other work that needs to be done.

Eliminating over-processing, or the excessive addition of any component in a workload or production despite not necessary prevents unnecessary expenses. It also conserves time and energy.

Kanban

The next chapter will be talking about situations wherein you can improve your managing skills with the help of Kanban, Lean Thinking, Agile, and Scrum. Being in you're A-Game will surely lead your whole team into success in the future.

Chapter 6. Using Visualization Tools To Lead Your People To Success

Managing your people is not an easy task and issues in the business make things a lot worse. You'll need the right tools to deal with various issues. Implementing Kanban, Lean Thinking, Agile, and Scrum to your business will aid you in those endeavors.

Using the Kanban method

Kanban is a method used for workflow management which is designed to help you to visualize the work you have and maximize the efficiency of the work you are doing all the while being agile in doing the work. A Kanban board can have as many columns depending on the process of work you are planning to do. The simplest form contains three columns - Requested, In Progress, Done.

Kanban

Key Performance Indicators aid you by providing criteria that determine whether the performances in the business are going well or not. Unfortunately, some companies do not apply these indicators in the business and some are not able to monitor these indicators. Either way, it causes these companies a lot of money, resources, and time.

By placing your projects in a Kanban board and setting up a limit in the "In Progress" column, you will be able to multitask projects. As long as you set up a limit in the "In Progress" column, which is based on the amount of work your team can handle at the moment, it is likely that the work will be done at the projected deadline you set. Additionally, Kanban's flexibility allows you to still point out problems that need to be addressed despite you are handling several projects at one time.

Identifying problems in your business can be easier through setting up your projects in a Kanban board. In a manufacturing setup, you will be able to see the bigger picture and identify the issues, be it knowing what causes the delay in the production of the item you sell or learn whether the overall process of producing your product is efficient. In an office setup, you will know as to what causes your team to not meet their deadlines, or you will be able to create a better-standardized process of dealing with projects since you have learned the previous one does not work efficiently.

Seeing the bigger picture lets you see what goes well and what needs improvement or change. Using the Kanban method in your business helps your team work out efficiently and maximize the output of your work. With that, you will be assured that everything goes well for your business.

Implementing Lean Thinking

Taiichi Ohno's original seven wastes can be eliminated if everyone in your company is adept in lean thinking.

Transportation can be prevented both in a manufacturing setup and in an office-based setup through different means. Workers who are working together in a project in an office-based environment should be close together. In a manufacturing setup, materials that are needed for the production of an item should be placed near the location of the production. In a manufacturing setup, transportation wastes can also be eliminated by setting up a U-shape production line, which creates a flow between the processes and also prevents overproducing work-in-progress products.

Excess inventory can be prevented whether you are working in an office or a manufacturing plant. You should only purchase raw materials when it is needed in the production, especially if the quantity of the raw materials is not enough for the production to proceed. By doing so, you can prevent work delays between production steps due to the excess amount of materials that need to be utilized.

Aside from purchasing materials only when necessary, you should also create a queue system. Having a queue system prevents the chances of overproduction to take place in your business.

Motion wastes include any movements of people, equipment, or machinery that are unnecessary. To prevent this, you should make sure that the workspace, be it in an office or a factory is well organized. Additionally, materials and equipment should be placed at ergonomic positions to reduce stretching and straining. In a manufacturing plant, equipment should always be placed near the location of the production.

Waiting wastes can be eliminated by designing a process, wherein the process guarantees the flow of the production to be continuous. Another way is through leveling the workload in the business by utilizing a set of standardized work instructions. It can also be through the development of workers that are flexible and possess multiple skills, that are also capable to adjust quickly to the demands of the work provided to them.

One way of eliminating overproduction is by time takt thinking. By calculating the ratio of the time of open production to the average consumer demand, you will know the needed capacity to have the flow of production to be steady.

Kanban

Through takt time thinking, you will be able to make sure that the manufacturing rate throughout the stations is even. Another way of eliminating overproduction is to reduce the time needed to set up everything and by doing so enables a continuous flow of the process. Additionally, by having a pull system, like Kanban, can prevent overproduction by controlling the number of Work-In-Progress projects being handled at the moment.

Over-processing can be eliminated just by simply understanding the work requirements based on the customer's perspective. Before starting your work, you should always bear a customer in mind, producing the item or doing the job at the level of expectation and quality the customer desires. Also, only produce items at the specified amount by the customers.

Defects can be eliminated is to look for the most common defect and give it more focus. You should identify what causes it to happen frequently. Then, provide solutions that prevent the defect to happen again during production.

Another thing that you can do to eliminate defects is by making sure that no defective items pass through the production process. You can do that by designing a process that determines abnormalities that can be found in the production. With that, you will be able to prevent more defects that can come out later in the production process.

Redesigning your process is another way of eliminating defects. By designing a process that takes into consideration the defects that may arise, you will be able to save money, time, and resources that may be wasted due to the defects that may occur. Using standardized work guarantees a consistent manufacturing process. Having standardized work guarantees that the overall process is defect free.

By eliminating wastes, you can be guaranteed that you are working efficiently. By training everyone in your business in applying lean thinking in daily business, you can be assured that the work that needs to be done not only will be done at the projected deadline, but it also does not cost you unnecessary resources, energy, and money.

Maintaining an Agile environment

An agile environment helps everyone in your company design and build the right product that is demanded by the consumers. By its iterative approach, you are allowed to analyze and improve the product you are working on throughout its development. Having an agile environment enables your business to produce a high-value product that will let you stay competitive in today's market.

Retaining loyal customers is hard nowadays, especially since in every type of business you will not only deal with the ever-changing demands by the consumers but also you will have to deal with emerging competitors. Through disciplined project management, items are regularly inspected and adapted corresponding to the feedback from the consumers. With that, the assurance of products made with quality is ensured. Quality products not only retain loyal customers, but they can also attract potential customers.

Demands by customers change throughout time and it can be a hard thing to deal with. Having an agile environment, however, makes it easier to deal with. Accepting changes in requirements no matter be it early or late in the project it was asked is one of the principles in Agile. Despite how hard it is, training and working in an agile environment develop the whole team to adapt to changes asked by customers.

One of the problems faced in companies is the lack of leadership which greatly affects the performance of the team. Through the application of and training of leaders with Agile, leadership philosophies that promote teamwork will be embodied by the leaders which will surely boost up team performance. Teams working together and lead by efficient leaders make tasks easier to accomplish.

Applying the Scrum Framework

Remember that a Scrum team consists of three roles, the Product Owner, the Development Team, and the Scrum Master. The supervisor or the manager is usually given the role of either the Product Owner or the Scrum Master. Both roles have different tasks in a Scrum environment, however, both roles are fundamental to the success of the Scrum.

The Product Owner has the responsibility of the work of the development team and the maximization of the value of the product the Scrum team is working on. He or she is also responsible for managing the product backlog. Their job includes expressing clearly the items in the Product backlog, achieving the goals and missions through ordering items in the Product backlog, optimizing the value of work the Development Team is working on, and making sure that the Product Backlog is transparent, visible, and clear to everyone.

The Scrum Master, on the other hand, is responsible for making sure that everyone in the team understands and puts into action the

Scrum theory, practices and rules. He or she works as the servant-leader for the team through guiding them as to how they incorporate the Scrum daily. He also guides the people who are not part of the Scrum team as to which of their interactions with the team helps and which do not.

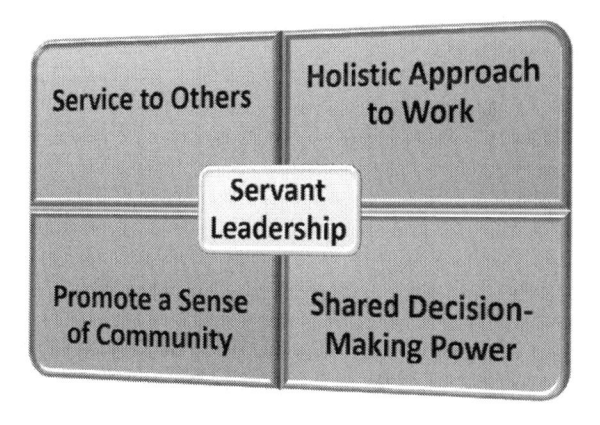

Service to Others	Holistic Approach to Work
Promote a Sense of Community	Shared Decision-Making Power

Servant Leadership

Balancing the growth of the company and the quality of work done by the employees is a headache if not managed properly. Growing companies tend to neglect one of the two while focusing on the other, which leads to several other problems later on. These problems include inefficiency, backlogs, low quality work offered,

Kanban

and the inability to keep up with the ever-changing customer demands in the market.

Through the Product Owner and the Scrum Master, the quality of the work being produced by the team will not suffer as the executive level management focuses on the growth of the company. The Product Owner provides the work requirements to the development team, making sure that the development team works on the product having in mind the requirements demanded by the customers. The Scrum Master guarantees that the Development Team and the Product Owner do their corresponding tasks at their maximum potential through encouragement and guidance of the whole Scrum framework.

Chapter 7. How To Kanbanize Your Workplace And Develop Your Employees

Agha Hasan Abedi once said, "The conventional definition of management is getting work done through people, but real management is developing people through work."

Employees contribute a big percentage to the success or the downfall of the business, depending on how you handle them. By training, encouragement, and engagement to your employees daily, you guarantee the brighter future of your business.

By training everyone in the company, everyone will eventually make their contribution in the identification and elimination of waste. It will not happen overnight, but there will be improvement day by day, little by little.

Training For Managers

Senior management and middle management should be trained regarding the importance of how things operate from the frontlines. They should have a firsthand experience of what is happening in the workplace. They are tasked to find out the facts themselves, and not only rely on reports submitted during boardroom meetings.

Engaging with the front-line employees and their work should be regularly done by the supervisors and managers to get a full grasp of the situation. By doing so, they can think and offer solutions to these problems as quickly as possible. It is also by them spending time at the workplace and with the employees that they can point out factors that may contribute to problems that may arise later on.

If you are a manager or supervisor, being able to point out bottlenecks in the process will save time, energy, and resources that might be allocated for the process had these bottlenecks were not pointed out earlier. The energy, time, and resources that were saved can then be used for other processes.

Fixing Skill Mismatch

Given the ability to visualize the overall and each specific part of the workflow, you can identify bottlenecks that can affect the work progress. There are occasions that these bottlenecks come from employees. It may be caused by them not being properly oriented of their tasks or how the equipment works, a mismatch between their skills and the tasks handed to them, absenteeism, and many more.

One of the bottlenecks that may arise in the process is the lack of knowledge of some employees of the older generation with new technologies present in society. Assigning them to other tasks that they are capable of at the moment is the best way to go. At the same time, you should train them to handle these new technologies introduced to the business.

Teaching them new things improve their performance and capabilities. Older generation employees work their selves out with full dedication to your company. Helping them improve their work by maximizing their capabilities will boost their confidence, shows them that you trust them, and surely will increase your sales later on.

Quality circles

This refers to a team of people who work on similar tasks. These groups are formed in order to discuss problems with the workflow particularly quality issues and to develop solutions for improvement. They're usually small and are led by a mentor. Ideally, they are given training in problem solving methods like brainstorming and cause-and-effect diagrams. They will present their findings and recommendations to management and when solutions are approved, these teams will be handling the implementation.

Kaizen spirit

Kaizen operates on the principle that improvement is a normal part of a job, and it is not something you only do when there is only available time after you've done everything else. Quality circles and individual suggestions can help improve the work within the normal working day. Encourage employees to be on the lookout for ways in which the system can be improved. Be open to suggestions. One of the ways in which this can be implemented is by making use of Andon.

Andon, a Japanese word used in the lean production approach, is a system of notifying the management, other workers, and maintenance of problems concerning quality or process. It can be through manual activation of a worker through a button or pull cord and can be also automatically activated by the production equipment itself. The work will be stopped until the problem is solved.

Most businesses utilize software or machines to do work. Despite having these things, automated work still needs specified human judgment to have things done the right way. With that, a lot of machines cannot be left alone to do the work provided since there's a possibility that things could go wrong if no one monitors them.

The practice of continuous imparting of human judgment to the system so that the system can monitor by itself without the unnecessary calling out of a human whenever it feels there is something wrong is known as automation. It is important since it separates the people from the machines, and prevents humans from doing the work tasked to the machines. It teaches lean thinking everyone in the company to look for ways to design smarter and lighter machines that cost less on capital expenditure.

Implementing lean thinking in the workplace means promoting the idea that everyone thinking together and that no one should be left with a problem to face alone. The practice of Andon enables knowledgeable employees to stop the production of a product once a defect is identified and call for assistance to resolve the issue. Andon teaches lean thinking to employees by pointing out on-the-spot obstacles to the lean aim of having zero defects at all stages of the process throughout the entire process, at all times.

Use the PDCA technique

This is an acronym for Plan-Do-Check-Act, the four steps in the iterative management approach developed by William Edwards Deming, an American statistician who spent time in Japan to train leaders of notable businesses. It can be used a problem solving technique.

Let's say that you're facing a major issue with how fast your customer support team can handle complaints. Many customers are unhappy with how much time it takes for them to receive any response. Here's how you can use PDCA to try to solve the problem

1. Plan. In this stage, you do just that – develop a plan for what needs to be done. If it's a large project, chances are, planning alone will take a lot of time and effort. You can make this undertaking manageable by taking smaller steps or

dividing it into manageable chunks. In this stage, you will need to identify the core issues that need to be resolved, the resources you already have, and the resources you will need to acquire. In the event that it's not possible to acquire certain resources you also need to create a plan about what you can do with what's available.

You also need to set the "win condition." This refers to a concrete goal that would allow you to know outright if your plan is working. For example, your win condition could be that "Only 3% of customer complains mention slow response rate as a problem" or "10 work hours have been spent on customer support".

Go through the plan with your entire team a couple of times before you start the next stage.

2. Do. In this stage, you apply everything that has been discussed in the previous stage. It's best to implement your plan on

a small scale because unpredicted problems may still arise.

For example, if the problem is the rate at which customer concerns are handled and during the planning stage, you have determined that it's because there is no workforce that is dedicated for this task, consider training a few of your employees to allocate more time to customer support instead of building an entire customer support department. Keep in mind that this will have repercussions on your entire system because the time allocated for customer support will be removed from existing tasks.

3. Check. This is a crucial phase of the PDCA process. Audit how the plan was executed and check if it actually worked. Check if the win condition has occurred. Did the amount of customers complaining about slow response decrease? If it did, you still need to check if the number of customer complaints is actually the same in comparison to previous numbers. Did the

employees really spend more time on customer support? Perhaps, there was a reduction in complaints because business was slow in the first place. Perhaps, the employees really did increase the amount of time they spend on customer support but it wasn't enough.

You need to know if the problem has been resolved and if it wasn't, you need to analyze it and pinpoint the root cause.

Act. If everything seems to have worked out, it's time to apply your initial plan on a larger scale.

The next time you face an issue about customer support, you can go through all these steps again and make small changes.

The PDCA cycle is a powerful tool for fixing problems at any level in your organization. And because it's iterative, your team can keep on finding and testing solutions over time and make small improvements. Just keep in mind that it takes time so it's not ideal to use this method to deal with an urgent problem.

SMED

SMED, which was originally known as Single Minute Exchange of Die or the changing of tools under ten minutes, is a fundamental practice in lean thinking which directly focuses on flexibility.

Flexibility is the ability to quickly switch from one project to another. SMED teaches lean thinking by seeking to improve flexibility all the time until a continuous flow at the right order which can respond to immediate demands by customers.

Standardized Work

Standardized work refers to the graphical illustration of the smooth flow with zero or one work-in-progress and having a clear location for everything including steps. This can help when implementing lean thinking management methods. After all, lean thinking is all about going for the smoothest workflow in every project through identifying and resolving problems one by one, leading to the development

Kanban

of both the workflow and the autonomy of the employees.

When there is standardized work, you are providing your employees guidelines on how work is executed. However, over time, these guidelines would have to be updated due to the nature of Agile development. Changes occur and improvements are made, and you need to make sure that the entire team is on board. When a team member is lagging and a bottleneck is form in the parts of the board that he is working on, the entire team will be effected.

Here are some steps in making sure that standardized work is practiced in an Agile environment.

1. Prioritize the routines that directly add value to your process – the things that affect quality and production speed. Of course, there are things that do not add value but must still be complied with, such as safety standards.

2. Develop best practices for executing tasks. This can be done through workshops with the staff. The routine should be as clear as possible and the recommended processing time for each step should be indicated. Include checkpoints that employees could use to be aware of deviations. Test to make sure that the guidelines or instructions are reasonable,.
3. Present the task and flow in visual form. This is were Kanban boards can come in handy. Employees and managers should be able to tell outright what needs to be done and whether it's getting done properly. This can also make it easier to check what can be improved.
4. Training every team member to the standard. Make sure that everyone knows they're expected to follow the guidelines. Make it clear that you want everyone to raise a signal immediately if a problem arises.
5. Team leaders should be aware that they're expected to initiate improvement work. It's best to standardize certain aspects of

the manager's tasks as well. A manager should always consider whether there's anything that will hinder the work flow for a specific day.
6. Utilize an improvement process. The board could use indicators that a task has been performed to standard. For example, green cards can be used to indicate that something went smoothly, and red could indicate that there was deviation. This way, you could spot problems that recur. Conduct meetings regularly to talk about problems and improvements.

Standardized work allows employees to identify tricky quality points such that they can visualize which matters to the customer, able to distinguish what goes right or wrong at every stage, and can confidently proceed from one stage to another. It teaches employees lean thinking through the visualization of every hindrance to the smoothness of the work and pointing out topics for Kaizen.

Consider training your employees with lean thinking so they can improve their skills and capabilities, which then can be used to identify and resolve issues in the business. When used with the application of the Agile Manifesto, overall performance will be improved. When the Scrum Framework is integrated into your system, it allows work to be easier through the members of the scrum teams having their specific roles and contribution to the success of the project.

Conclusion

I'd like to thank you and congratulate you for transiting my lines from start to finish. I hope this book was able to help you to visualize the overall workflow and maximize the efficiency and output of the overall work process through the application of Kanban, Lean Thinking, Agile, and Scrum to your business.

Kanban is a method that gives you the ability to visualize the overall workflow and spot problems that hinder the progress of the workflow. This is done through various techniques such as standardized work and the use of indicators such as lead time and cycle time.

To maximize the efficiency of the process and achieve the output goal you have in mind, you should make sure that the overall workflow goes smoothly. With the use of the Kanban board and cards, you will be able to get a good picture of the workflow, which gives you then the idea of which processes work well and which processes have problems.

Kanban also maximizes efficiency by enabling your team to multitask to an extent. Multitasking can do harm when done poorly so kanban places a limit on the work-in-progress, which depends on the capability of the workers and the capacity of the equipment. With the limit present, you will also be allowed to work in a sustainable manner. This also boosts employee morale.

As a lean thinking tool, Kanban promotes the identification and elimination of waste, resulting to more profits. The fact that lean thinking encourages managers to focus on the frontlines and develop the employees also help maintain morale and create an environment that promotes accountability and productivity. The regular workplace visits enables them to stay attuned to what's going on and what can be done to make sure that the workflow goes smoothly.

As an agile development technique, it also helps you keep customers satisfied, thanks to the flexibility that it allows and the pace with which it can keep up with customer's demands.

The next step for you to do is to apply what you have learned here in your business. By doing so, it will be a guarantee that you will be able to visualize every aspect of the workflow, assuring the smooth flow of the process. By having a smooth flow, you will then maximize the efficiency of the work being done, and finally, maximize the output quality to the levels demanded by the consumers.

If there is one thing that I want to happen, that is the success of your business through the tips provided in this book. Start making assessments in your business and apply the things you learned in this book and secure the success of your business in the coming days. I wish you the best of luck!

Thank you

Before you go, I just wanted to say thank you for purchasing my book.

You could have picked from dozens of other books on the same topic but you took a chance and chose this one.

So, a HUGE thanks to you for getting this book and for reading all the way to the end.

Now I wanted to ask you for a small favor. ***Could you please consider posting a review on the platform? Reviews are one of the easiest ways to support the work of independent authors.***

This feedback will help me continue to write the type of books that will help you get the results you want. So if you enjoyed it, please let me know!

REFERENCES

Agile Vs Scrum: Know the Difference. (2019, September 21). Retrieved November 4, 2019, from https://www.guru99.com/agile-vs-scrum.html

Amjal, S. (2018, May 4). How Agile Scrum Training Transformed These 5 Companies. Retrieved November 4, 2019, from https://www.quickstart.com/blog/how-agile-scrum-training-transformed-these-5-companies/

Goldman, L.,Nagel, R.L., & Preiss, K. (1995). Agile Competitors and Virtual Organizations - Strategies for Enriching the Customer, *Van Nostrand Reinhold.*

Gonçalves, L. (2019a, September 16). What is Scrum Methodology, Everything You Need To Know About. Retrieved November 4, 2019, from https://luis-goncalves.com/what-is-scrum-methodology/

Gonçalves, L. (2019b, October 5). What Is Agile Methodology. Retrieved November 4, 2019, from https://luis-goncalves.com/what-is-agile-methodology/

Highsmith, J. (2001a). History: The Agile Manifesto. Retrieved November 4, 2019, from https://agilemanifesto.org/history.html

Highsmith, J. (2001b). Principles behind the Agile Manifesto. Retrieved November 4, 2019, from https://agilemanifesto.org/principles.html

Jansson, K. (2017, May 2). "Lean Thinking" and the 5 Principles of Lean Manufacturing. Retrieved November 4, 2019, from https://blog.kainexus.com/improvement-disciplines/lean/lean-thinking-and-the-5-principles-of-lean-manufacturing

Kanban Explained in 10 Minutes | Kanbanize. (n.d.). Retrieved November 4, 2019, from https://kanbanize.com/kanban-resources/getting-started/what-is-kanban/

Landeghem, L. (2015, January 4). Why is Overproduction the Worst Muda? |. Retrieved

November 4, 2019, from http://www.consulting-xp.com/blog/?p=546

Leading Edge Group. (2018, October 12). Key Performance Indicators for Production Monitoring - Leading Edge. Retrieved November 4, 2019, from https://www.leadingedgegroup.com/key-performance-indicators-for-production-monitoring/

Lotich, P. (2014, October 7). Internal Problems Can Impact Your Customers - Are You Aware? – The Thriving Small Business. Retrieved November 4, 2019, from https://thethrivingsmallbusiness.com/small-business-problems/

Mathew, A. (2015, April 20). The Impact of a Poor Customer Service. Retrieved November 4, 2019, from https://www.liveadmins.com/blog/the-impact-of-a-poor-customer-service/

Naydenov, P. (2019a, October 10). Top Reasons Why Companies Use Kanban [Infographic]|Kanbanize Blog. Retrieved

November 4, 2019, from https://kanbanize.com/blog/why-use-kanban-infographic/

Naydenov, P. (2019b, October 11). Kanban in IT Operations: 5 Real-Life Examples. Retrieved November 4, 2019, from https://kanbanize.com/blog/kanban-it-operations/

Ohno, T. (June 1988). Toyota Production System - beyond large-scale production. Productivity Press. p. 29. ISBN 0-915299-14-3.

Peshev, M. (2019, February 23). The 31 Biggest Business Challenges Growing Companies Face - Mario Peshev. Retrieved November 4, 2019, from https://mariopeshev.com/business/the-biggest-business-challenges-growing-companies/

Schonberger, R.J. (2001). Let's Fix It! Overcoming the Crisis in Manufacturing. New York: Free Press. pp. 70–71.

Shingō, S. (1989). A Study of the Toyota Production System from an Industrial

Engineering Viewpoint. Productivity Press. p. 228. ISBN 0-915299-17-8.

Skhmot, N. (2017, August 5). The 8 Wastes of Lean. Retrieved November 4, 2019, from https://theleanway.net/The-8-Wastes-of-Lean

Smartsheet. (n.d.). Understanding Kanban Inventory Management and Its Uses Across Multiple Industries. Retrieved November 21, 2019, from https://www.smartsheet.com/understanding-kanban-inventory-management-and-its-uses-across-multiple-industries

The Leadership Network. (2015, November 10). How Kanban systems are used in different industries. Retrieved November 21, 2019, from https://theleadershipnetwork.com/article/kanban

Top 10: Lean manufacturing companies in the world. (2017, April 26). Retrieved November 4, 2019, from https://www.manufacturingglobal.com/top-10/top-10-lean-manufacturing-companies-world

What is Agile/Scrum. (2019, October 22). Retrieved November 4, 2019, from https://www.cprime.com/resources/what-is-agile-what-is-scrum/

Womack, J. P. & Jones, D.T. (1996) Lean Thinking.

Womack, J. P., Jones, D.T. & Roos, D. (1990) The Machine That Changed The World.

Printed in Great Britain
by Amazon